Pieced Clothing

# VARIATIONS

by

## Yvonne Porcella

Photography by Elaine F. Keenan

Published by Porcella Studios
3619 Shoemake Ave.
Modesto, CA 95351
(209) 524-1134

# Table of Contents

Since 1976 I have been experimenting with my own costume designs based on traditional folk clothing styles. The response to the pattern books that resulted from my study has been tremendous. *FIVE ETHNIC PATTERNS* and *PLUS FIVE* were the first two pattern booklets printed and they continue to appeal to a large audience. *PIECED CLOTHING* book written in 1980 included color photos of patterns in the book which were designed with piecing and patchwork.

Now I offer you *VARIATIONS* which again is a progression of all that has come before. In *VARIATIONS* I have chosen one basic pattern with shaped shoulder seams and adapted it to be made in different ways.

The principle of construction remains the same in *VARIATIONS* as in *PIECED CLOTHING*. Most pattern pieces are cut from a rectangle. This type of construction allows the sewer to cut directly into the fabric without the aid of a pattern. Each pattern piece as a flat shape can be embellished before the garment is assembled.

I have included very brief instructions which outline my approach to strip piecing and patchwork. It has been my assumption that most of my readers are skilled craftsmen and have their own personal ideas of how to embellish my patterns. For that reason I leave the designing of the garment surface up to you the reader. I provide a quick, easy pattern and method for construction.

## GENERAL DIRECTIONS

Prewash fabrics before cutting. Cotton, cotton blends and silk fabrics are recommended for use in these patterns.

If underlining is suggested in pattern directions, use cotton flannel, muslin, or broadcloth. Underlining is foundation for strip piecing; it gives the garment a better shape, and it discourages wrinkling.

All patterns in this book call for a 1/4" seam allowance. All pattern pieces have two or three layers—patchwork, underlining or batting, and lining where indicated. Try to be accurate and trim pattern pieces carefully so all layers will be even and caught in the machine seam. Seams with binding are seven layers thick. A 1/4" seam is adequate but personal preference is allowed. If desired, cut pattern pieces larger for a wider seam allowance.

## INSTRUCTIONS FOR BINDING

If pattern calls for binding to cover raw edges in garment, use a self made binding. Binding can be cut from the fabrics you are working with or use a contrasting fabric for added color.

All straight edge seams use a straight grain fabric binding. All curved seams use a bias binding. All binding is cut 1-1/2" wide and is sewn with a 1/4" seam.

With right sides together pin binding to garment seams matching raw edges. Sew binding and garment seams together. There is no need to sew seams first and then sew binding on top. This adds extra weight to a narrow seam. Press binding over machine sewn seam. Fold in raw edge of binding to meet raw edge of seam. Fold binding again and pin over machine seam line. Slip stitch folded edge of binding over machine seam line.

## HOW TO CHANGE PATTERN SIZE

The patterns in this book are shown in medium size. Use following directions to make a smaller or larger size for personal fit.

Measure around bust with a tape measure. To bust measurement add two or more inches for garment ease. This adjusted bust measurement will be divided among the pattern pieces.

Hold tape measure across upper chest. Look in the mirror to determine the width of your center panel. Tape should be positioned from inside left armhole to inside right armhole.

The center panel provides both the front and back of the pattern. Take center panel front measurement plus the same width for the back panel and subtract from your adjusted bust measurement. The answer is the amount needed for the side panels. Divide the answer in half to determine the width of each side panel.

For waist length, measure from shoulder to waist to determine length of center panel. Depth of armhole is measured from shoulder to underarm. Allow an extra one to two inches for ease underarm. Subtract armhole depth from length of center panel to determine length of side panel. Add 1/4" seam allowance to all pieces before cutting.

To measure for shaped shoulder seam, hold a ruler flat against neck where shoulder meets neck. Measure the distance between ruler and tip of shoulder. Medium size is 1-1/4" drop from ruler to tip of shoulder. Angle shoulder seam on pattern from neck opening to tip of shoulder. Allow 1/4" seam allowance to pattern before cutting. See drawing to measure for shaped shoulder seam on page 38.

## STRIP PIECING

All straight grain strips of fabric for piecing are cut from 45″ wide fabric. Press fabric and fold in half (22-1/2″ wide) matching selvages. Use a C-THRU ruler (18″ by 2″) or straight template to draw accurate lines of various widths on fabric. Draw with chalk. Cut fabric on drawn lines as accurately as possible. Use a carpenter's square to help mark lines on fabric. This is a right angle ruler purchased at hardware stores for about $6.00. The ruler is 16″ by 24″. Place one side of ruler on fold of fabric. The other side of the ruler will be an accurate straight line across the fabric. Keep ruler in place and use C-THRU ruler to measure width of strips using measurements on right angle ruler to help insure accuracy.

Begin garment by selecting various colors of prints and solid fabric. Five different colors is an easy number to work with although sample garments in this book have many more colors.

Cut varying width strips of fabric from all your colors (1-1/2″ wide, 2″ wide, 3″ wide, etc.). Have strips ready at hand to select during piecing process. If you cut too many strips they can always be used in another project.

An underlining serves as a foundation for sewing the strips of fabric in place in machine piecing. Begin by pinning one strip of fabric to underlining. Take a second strip and place it right sides together on top of first strip. Each strip should extend to outside edges of underlining. Pin strips in place and seam on one side. Sew through the two strips of fabric and the underlining. Open second strip and press right side up. Continue in this way to piece across the whole underlining.

Strips can themselves be pieced before sewing onto underlining. For instance, cut five colors of fabric into 2″ wide strips. Sew together along the 45″ wide length with 1/4″ seams. Press seams all going in one direction. The result is a "new" piece of fabric which measures 8″ wide by 45″ long. Put C-THRU ruler on top of 8″ wide fabric matching up horizontal lines on ruler with seams. Mark a line vertically with chalk every 2″. Cut on vertical lines. Sew this 2″ pieced strip in with other strips on underlining. Be sure pieced strip is long enough to extend to outside edges of underlining.

Making a checkerboard is done in the same way as piecing strips. Two contrasting colors of fabric are cut into strips such as 2″ by 45″. Sew together with 1/4″ seams alternating colors (red, black, red, black). Begin with one color and end with the other. Cut this "new" fabric into four 2″ strips and turn every other piece opposite to have alternating squares of color. Sew strips together to make checkerboard.

## PATCHWORK

The term patchwork in this book refers to sewing small pieces of fabric together to make a large piece of cloth. Each pattern piece of a garment is then cut from a large piece of patchwork cloth. The garment pattern piece is then batted and lined. All three layers are hand quilted before assembling into wearable garment. Personal choice of patchwork can be used in the patterns in this book.

**A.  Short Sleeve Coat**
*Over the Rainbow.* Strip pieced to underlining.
Pattern on page 34.

# Basic Vest

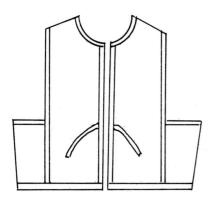

This is a waist length vest pattern. It is the basic pattern from which all other patterns in the book were developed. This vest can be made in one fabric, batted with a commercial batting, lined and machine quilted as in the vest shown on page 12. Or the vest can be made in strip piecing to an underlining and lined as in the vest shown on page 12. The vest pattern consists of a center panel front and back and two side panels.

TO DETERMINE FABRIC NEEDED: the vest is waist length and can be made from 1/2 yard of fabric for the outside and 1/2 yard of fabric for the lining. An additional 1/2 yard of fabric is needed for the bias binding to cover raw edges. If the vest is batted, 1/2 yard of 45″ wide batting is needed. For a strip pieced vest use 1/2 yard of underlining. See General Directions. Small amounts of different fabrics for piecing are needed. See directions for strip piecing on page 4.

TO DETERMINE VEST SIZE: the measurements in this book are for a medium size. To change the pattern size for personal fit follow directions on page 3.

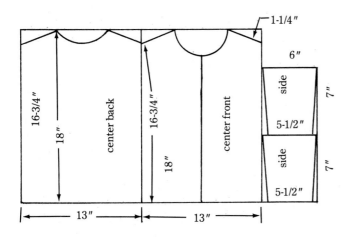

dimensions of pattern pieces

DIMENSIONS OF PATTERN PIECES: center panel has front and back panel 13″ wide by 18″ long sewn together at the shoulder. Shape shoulder seam 1-1/4″. Add 1/4″ seam allowance to pattern piece for shoulder seam. Neck opening is from template found in back of book. It is finished with a bias binding. No seam allowance is necessary on neck edge. Armhole is 9″ from shoulder seam to top of side panel. Side panel length is 9″ shorter than center panel. Width of side panel is 6″ wide by 7″ long. Side panel can be shaped to allow for narrower look at waistline. Medium is 6″ at top and 5-1/2″ at bottom and 7″ long.

ADD 1/4″ SEAM ALLOWANCE

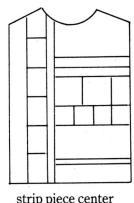

strip piece center back

Cut out center panel for a strip pieced vest by drawing a rectangle on the underlining fabric. Draw rectangle and then trace template for back neck opening in center of top edge. Shape shoulder by drawing from neck opening to armhole edge allowing 1/4″ seam allowance. Repeat for center front. Slash center front for front opening after drawing neck opening. Vest edges just meet in front. There is no overlap.

COVER CENTER BACK PANEL underlining with strip piecing. Line center back panel with lining fabric. Repeat piecing on center front underlining. Line center front panels.

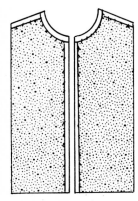

bind center front
sew shoulder seams
bind neck

BIND CENTER FRONT raw edges with straight grain binding. See instructions for binding on page 3. If ties are desired as front closure, add ties in binding seam. Ties are 6″ long and cut from 1-1/2″ wide strip of fabric finished to 1/2″ wide.

Sew shoulder seams. To finish shoulder seam, sew center back all three layers—pieced layer, underlining, lining. Sew to center front two layers—pieced layer, underlining. Hand sew the front panel lining over shoulder seam.

Finish neck opening with bias binding.

side panel

CUT TWO SIDE PANELS in underlining fabric and piece as for center panels. Line side panels. Finish top of side panels with straight grain binding.

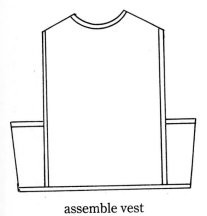

assemble vest

ASSEMBLE VEST by sewing side panels to center panel with bias binding over seam. Binding can be decorative on outside of vest or sewn on lining side. For outside binding pin with lining sides together. Pin side panels to center panel starting at waist edge. For inside binding pin with outsides together. This binding also finishes the armhole.

Finish lower edge of vest with straight grain binding.

NOTE: if using batting in the vest as pictured on page 12, follow directions for Basic Vest with Patchwork.

# Basic Vest with Patchwork

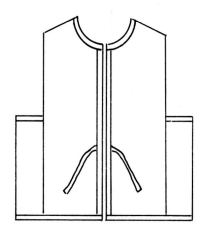

This vest is the same as the basic vest pattern except it is three inches longer. The sample vest as shown on page 29 is patchwork. Sew patches of fabric together until a rectangle is made the size of the pattern piece. Each part of the vest is then batted and lined. Hand quilting is done before vest is assembled.

TO DETERMINE FABRIC NEEDED: the vest can be made from scraps of fabric for the outside and 2/3 yard of fabric for the lining. Batting is needed. Use either a crib batt or as thin a batt as available. An additional 1/2 yard of fabric is needed for bias binding to cover raw edges.

TO DETERMINE VEST SIZE: the measurements in this book are for a medium size. To change the pattern size for personal fit follow directions on page 3.

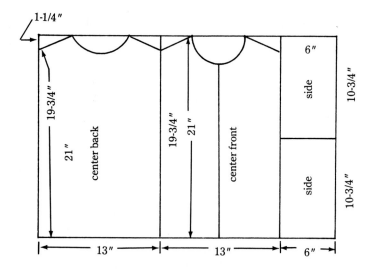

dimensions of pattern pieces

DIMENSIONS OF PATTERN PIECES: center panel has front and back panel 13" wide by 21" long sewn together at the shoulder. Shape shoulder seam 1-1/4". Add 1/4" seam allowance to pattern piece for shoulder seam. Neck opening is from template found in back of book. It is finished with a bias binding. No seam allowance is necessary on neck edge. Armhole is 9" from shoulder seam to top of side panel. Side panel length is 9" from shoulder seam to top of side panel. Side panel length is 9" shorter than center panel. Width of side panel is 6" wide by 10-3/4" long. Side panel is a rectangle. It may be necessary to enlarge the side panel at the lower edge in the longer vest to allow for body shaping below the waist. If personal measurements three inches below the waist is greater than measurement of center front plus center back plus two side panels, 13" + 13" + 6" + 6", shape the side panel at lower edge to add extra width necessary for fit.

ADD 1/4" SEAM ALLOWANCE

TO BEGIN VEST make patchwork large enough to make a rectangle the size of the center back, 13″ by 21″. Draw back neck opening from template and the shaped shoulder seam on patchwork piece. Cut out center back pattern piece. Cut batting the same shape. Cut lining. Pin all three layers together. Hand quilt through all three layers. Repeat for center fronts. Slash center front for front opening. Vest edges just meet in front. There is no overlap.

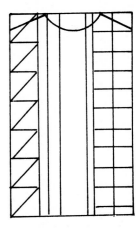

back panel

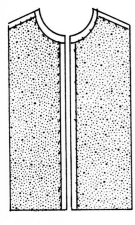

bind center front
sew shoulder seams
bind neck

BIND CENTER FRONT raw edges with straight grain binding. See General Directions on page 3. If ties are desired as front closure, add ties in the binding seam. Ties are 6″ long and cut from 1-1/2″ wide strip of fabric finished to 1/2″ wide.

Sew shoulder seams. To finish shoulder seam raw edge, sew a piece of binding over shoulder seam. Hand sew binding over machine seam.

Finish neck opening with bias binding.

SIDE PANELS are cut from two rectangles of patchwork. Cut two side panels from patchwork 6″ by 10-3/4″. Batt side panels and line. Pin three layers together and hand quilt. Finish top of side panel with straight grain binding.

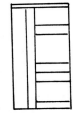

side panel

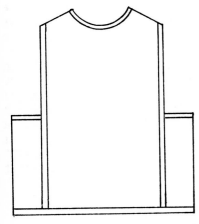

assemble vest

ASSEMBLE VEST by sewing side panels to center panel with bias binding over seam. Binding can be decorative on outside of vest or sewn on lining side. For outside binding pin with lining sides together. For inside binding, pin with outsides together. Pin side panels to center panel matching up lower edges of center panels and side panels. This binding also finishes the armhole.

Finish lower edge of vest with straight grain binding.

# Little Jacket

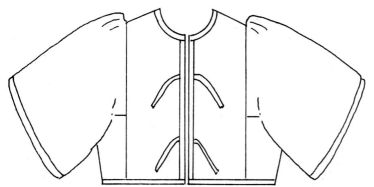

This little jacket is the basic vest pattern with full sleeves added to make a jacket. The sleeves are a rectangle gathered at shoulder. The jacket is strip pieced to an underlining. The sleeves are lined. See sample jacket on page 13.

TO DETERMINE FABRIC NEEDED: the little jacket is waist length and can be made from 1/2 yard of fabric for the outside, 1/2 yard of underlining and 1/2 yard of lining. Additional 1/2 yard is needed for bias binding to cover raw edges. Allow 2/3 yard of fabric for outside sleeve and 2/3 yard of fabric for sleeve lining. If jacket is strip pieced, small amounts of different fabrics for piecing are necessary. See directions for strip piecing on page 4.

TO DETERMINE JACKET SIZE: the measurements in this book are for a medium size. To change the pattern size for personal fit follow directions on page 3.

DIMENSIONS OF PATTERN PIECES: center panel has front and back panel 13" wide by 18" long sewn together at the shoulder. Shape shoulder 1-1/4". Add 1/4" seam allowance to pattern piece for shoulder seam. Neck opening is from template found in back of book. It is finished with a bias binding. No seam allowance is necessary on neck edge. Armhole is 9" from shoulder seam to top of side panel. Side panel length is 9" from shoulder seam to top of side panel. Side panel length is 9" shorter than center panel. Size of side panel is 6" wide by 7" long. Side panel can be shaped to allow for narrower look at waistline. Medium is 6" at top and 5-1/2" at bottom and 7" long. Sleeve is a rectangle 12" by 24". The sleeve is slightly gathered at shoulder to fit into 9" deep armhole.

ADD 1/4" SEAM ALLOWANCE

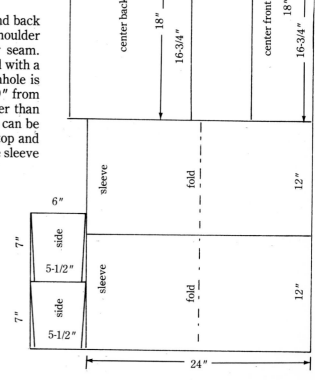

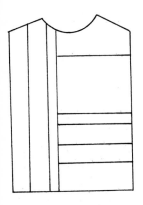

strip piece center
back

To cut out jacket begin with center panel back. Draw rectangle on underlining fabric. Draw rectangle and then trace template for back neck opening in center on top edge. Shape shoulder by drawing from neck opening to armhole edge allowing 1/4″ seam allowance. Repeat for center front. Slash center front for front opening after drawing neck opening. Jacket edges just meet in front. There is no overlap.

COVER CENTER BACK panel underlining with strip piecing. Line center back panel with lining fabric. Repeat piecing on center front underlining. Line center front panels.

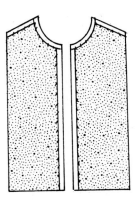

BIND CENTER FRONT raw edges with straight grain binding. See General Directions on page 3. If ties are desired as front closure, add ties in binding seam. Ties are 6″ long and cut from 1-1/2″ wide strip of fabric finished to 1/2″ wide.

Sew shoulder seams. To finish shoulder seam, sew center back all three layers—pieced layer, underlining, lining to center front two layers—pieced layer, underlining. Hand sew the front panel lining over shoulder seam.

Finish neck opening with bias binding.

bind center front
sew shoulder seams
bind neck

side panel

CUT TWO SIDE PANELS in underlining fabric and piece as for center panels. Line side panels. Do not finish top of side panel. Sleeve will be sewn to top of side panel in this jacket.

SLEEVES are two rectangles cut 12″ long by 24″ wide. The lining of the sleeve extends 1/4″ below the sleeve. Cut lining 1″ longer than sleeve, 13″ by 24″. Sleeve width can be altered. The sleeve is gathered at center and fitted into 9″ deep armhole. Sleeve can be made narrower by cutting sleeve 12″ long by 22″ wide. Sleeve is not underlined.

Sew sleeve and lining together along elbow edge. Press sleeve seam flat toward lining so lining will fold over seam allowance. With right sides together fold sleeve and lining on shoulder fold line.

Pattern continues on page 14.

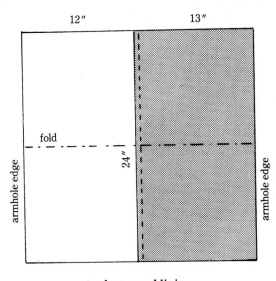

sew sleeve and lining

**B.**

**B.  Basic Vest**
*Wild Carnation.* One piece of
fabric batted and machine quilted.
Pattern on page 6.

**C.  Basic Vest**
*Color / Cloth.* Strip pieced to
underlining.
Pattern on page 6.

**C.**

**D.** **Little Jacket**
*Goosey Goosey Gander.* Strip pieced to underlining, lined sleeves.
Pattern on page 10.

Little Jacket continued.

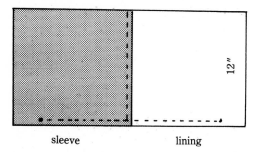

sew underarm seam

Sew underarm sleeve seam in center leaving both edges of sleeve and lining seam open.

LEAVE SEAM OPEN half the width of top of side panel. If side panel is 6″ at top, leave seam open 3″ on either end of underarm seam. Press seam open.

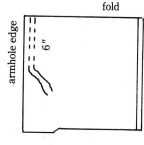

gather sleeve

TURN SLEEVE AND LINING so wrong sides are together. Pin armhole edge of sleeve and lining together. Mark shoulder fold line on sleeve. Sew two rows of machine gather stitches along armhole edge of sleeve for total of 12″ or 6″ on each side of shoulder fold line.

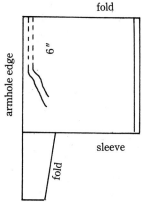

side panel and sleeve unit

SEW TOP OF SIDE PANEL to unsewn edge of underarm sleeve. *Sew side panel to sleeve fabric only.* Do not sew sleeve lining in this seam. Sleeve lining is *hand sewn* over machine seam to finish underarm seam. To sew seam, open underarm sleeve seam flat and pin top of side panel to sleeve seam. Stitch from each side of underarm seam to edge. Sew lining by hand over machine seam. See drawing.

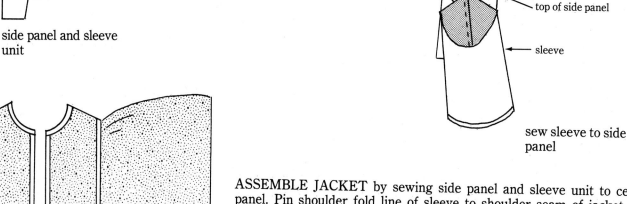

sew sleeve to side panel

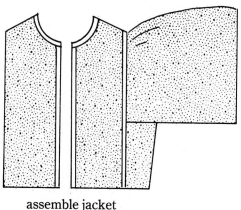

assemble jacket

ASSEMBLE JACKET by sewing side panel and sleeve unit to center panel. Pin shoulder fold line of sleeve to shoulder seam of jacket. Pin lower edge of side panel to lower edge of center panel. Continue pinning unit in place. Adjust gathers to fit sleeve into armhole. Sew bias binding over this joining seam.

Finish lower edge of jacket with straight grain binding.

# Half Circle Jacket

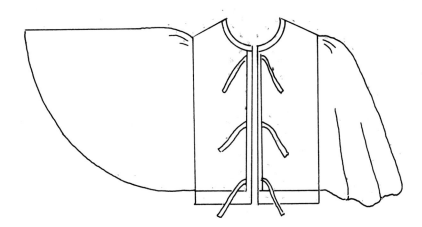

This jacket is the basic vest pattern with a half circle sleeve added. The sleeves are cut from a full circle of fabric with half making each sleeve. The diameter of the circle is joined to the jacket at the armhole edge. The jacket has a 1-1/2″ wide waist band trim. The sample jacket is silk strip pieced to an underlining. See sample jacket on page 20.

TO DETERMINE FABRIC NEEDED: the half circle jacket is waist length and can be made from 1/2 yard of fabric for the outside, 1/2 yard of underlining and 1/2 yard of lining. Additional 1/2 yard is needed for bias binding to cover raw edges. Allow one full yard of fabric for sleeves and one yard for optional sleeve lining. If jacket is done in strip piecing, small amounts of different fabrics for piecing are necessary. See directions for strip piecing on page 4.

TO DETERMINE JACKET SIZE: the measurements in this book are for a medium size. To change the pattern size for personal fit follow directions on page 3.

ADD 1/4″ SEAM ALLOWANCE

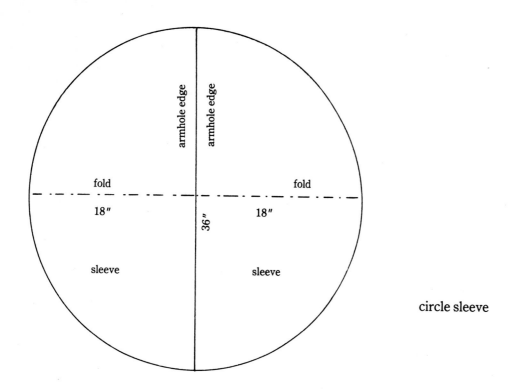

armhole edge

armhole edge

fold

fold

18″

18″

36″

sleeve

sleeve

circle sleeve

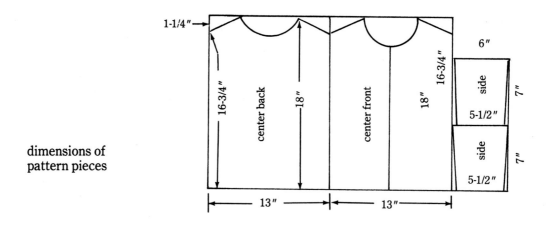

1-1/4″

16-3/4″

center back

18″

center front

18″

16-3/4″

6″

side

7″

5-1/2″

side

7″

5-1/2″

13″

13″

dimensions of
pattern pieces

DIMENSIONS OF PATTERN PIECES: center panel has front and back panel 13″ wide by 18″ long sewn together at the shoulder. Shape shoulder 1-1/4″. Add 1/4″ seam allowance to pattern piece for shoulder seam. Neck opening is from template found in back of book. It is finished with a bias binding. No seam allowance is necessary on neck edge. Armhole is 9″ from shoulder seam to top of side panel. Side panel length is 9″ shorter than center panel. Width of side panel is 6″ wide by 7″ long. Side panel can be shaped to allow for narrower look at waistline. Medium is 6″ at top and 5-1/2″ at bottom and 7″ long. Sleeve is a half circle 36″ on the diameter. The sleeve is slightly gathered at shoulder fold to fit into shaped armhole.

To cut out jacket begin with center panel back. Draw rectangle on underlining fabric. Draw rectangle and then trace template for back neck opening in center of top edge. Shape shoulder by drawing from neck opening to armhole edge allowing 1/4″ seam allowance. Repeat for center front. Slash center front for front opening after drawing neck opening. Jacket edges just meet in front. There is no overlap.

COVER CENTER BACK PANEL underlining with strip piecing. Line center back panel with lining fabric. Repeat piecing on center front underlining. Line front panels.

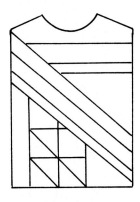

strip piece center back

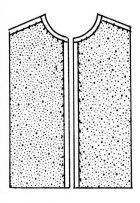

bind center front
sew shoulder seam
bind neck

BIND CENTER FRONT raw edges with straight grain binding. See General Directions on page 3. If ties are desired as front closure, add ties in binding seam. Ties are 6″ long and cut from 1-1/2″ wide strip of fabric finished to 1/2″ wide.

Sew shoulder seams. To finish shoulder seam, sew center back all three layers—pieced layer, underlining, lining to center front two layers—pieced layer, underlining. Hand sew front panel lining over shoulder seam.

Finish neck opening with bias binding.

CUT TWO SIDE PANELS in underlining fabric and piece as for center panels. Line side panels. Finish top of side panel with straight grain binding.

side panel

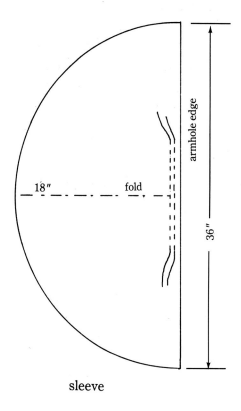

sleeve

SLEEVES ARE CUT from a circle 36″ on the diameter. Draw circle on a 36″ by 36″ piece of fabric. Cut circle in half. The diameter of the circle when cut will be the armhole edge of the sleeve and be sewn into the armhole edge of jacket. The sleeve may be lined with a very lightweight fabric. If so desired, cut sleeve lining the same size and sew sleeve and lining together along circular edge. Turn wrong sides together and press circular edge. Handle sleeve and lining as one fabric. Or the circular edge of the sleeve can be finished with a narrow hem and omit the lining.

Find center fold of sleeve along diameter. Mark and sew two rows of gather stitches for 12″ along sleeve armhole edge, that is 6″ on either side of center fold of sleeve.

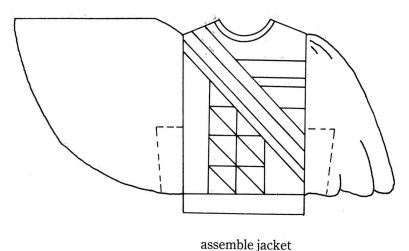

assemble jacket

ASSEMBLE JACKET by joining side panels to center panel putting 1/2 circle sleeve into seam. Sleeve on fold measures 18″. Pin center mark on sleeve to shoulder seam on jacket. Adjust gathers at shoulder and pin sleeve around armhole edge. Then pin side panel to center panel starting at lower edges. Sew armhole seam with bias binding over seam.

Finish lower edge of jacket with a 3-1/2″ wide band. Sew band to jacket edge. Fold band in half and fold in raw edge for 1/2″. Pin folded edge of band over machine seam. Slip stitch band to jacket edge. This makes a 1-1/2″ wide band on edge of jacket.

# Blouse

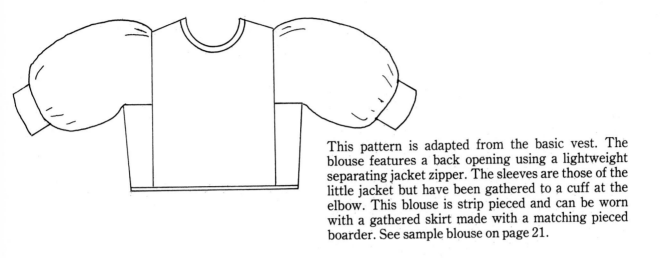

This pattern is adapted from the basic vest. The blouse features a back opening using a lightweight separating jacket zipper. The sleeves are those of the little jacket but have been gathered to a cuff at the elbow. This blouse is strip pieced and can be worn with a gathered skirt made with a matching pieced boarder. See sample blouse on page 21.

TO DETERMINE FABRIC NEEDED: the blouse is waist length and can be made from 1/2 yard of fabric for the outside and 1/2 yard of lightweight underlining. Blouse is not lined. Additional 2/3 yard for sleeve is needed plus 1/4 yard for cuffs. If blouse is done in strip piecing, small amounts of different fabrics are needed for piecing. See directions for strip piecing on page 4.

TO DETERMINE BLOUSE SIZE: the measurements in this book are for a medium size. To change pattern size for personal fit follow directions on page 3.

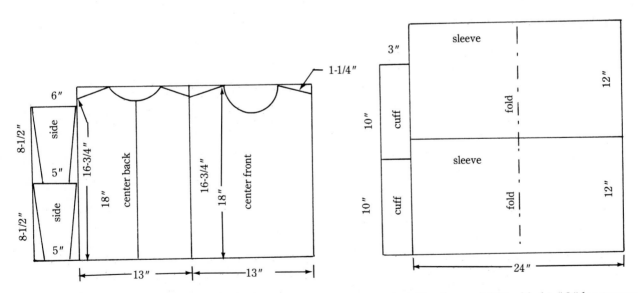

DIMENSIONS OF PATTERN PIECES: center panel has front and back panel 13″ wide by 18″ long sewn together at the shoulder. Shape shoulder 1-1/4″. Add 1/4″ seam allowance to pattern piece for shoulder seam. Neck opening is from template found in back of book. It is finished with a bias binding. No seam allowance is necessary on neck edge. Armhole is 8″ from shoulder seam to top of side panel. Side panel length is 8″ shorter than center panel. Size of side panel is 6″ wide by 8-1/2″ long. Side panel can be shaped to allow for narrower look at blouse waistline. Medium is 6″ at top and 5″ at bottom and 8-1/2″ long. Sleeve is a rectangle 12″ by 24″. The sleeve is slightly gathered at shoulder to fit into 8″ deep armhole. Cuff is 10″ by 3″. Cuff is lined.

ADD 1/4″ SEAM ALLOWANCE

Pattern continues on page 22.

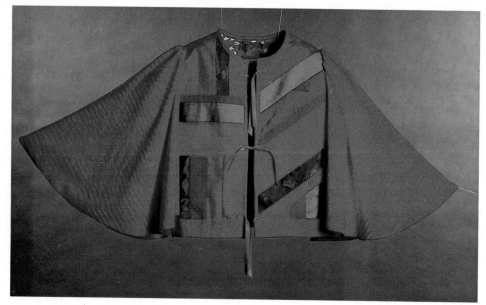

**E.**

**E.    Half Circle Jacket**
*Scarlet Ribbons.* Silk strip pieced
to underlining, lined sleeves.
Pattern on page 15.

**F.    Over Jacket**
*Prism.* Strip pieced to lining, lined
sleeves. Over Jacket can be worn
over Basic Vest.
Pattern on page 27.

**F.**

**G.**

**G.** **Long Sleeve Jacket**
*Topaz.* Strip pieced to underlining, unlined sleeves gathered to cuff. Pattern on page 24.

**H.**

**H.** **Blouse**
*Tekke.* Strip pieced to lining, unlined sleeves gathered to cuff. Chevron stripe hand pieced. Pattern on page 19.

Blouse continued.

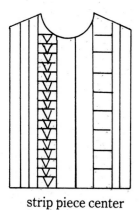

strip piece center
front

To cut out blouse begin with front panel. A lightweight underlining is used to support the piecing in sample blouse. Draw a rectangle on underlining fabric. Trace template for front neck opening on top edge of rectangle. Shape shoulder by drawing from neck opening to shoulder edge allowing 1/4″ seam allowance. Repeat for center back. Slash center back for back opening after drawing neck opening. Blouse opening edges meet in the back and a separating zipper is used as closure. Blouse is not lined.

COVER CENTER FRONT panel underlining with strip piecing. Repeat piecing on center back panel underlining.

BIND CENTER BACK opening raw edges with straight grain binding. See General Directions on page 3. Sew separating jacket zipper in back opening.

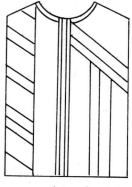

sew zipper in center
back

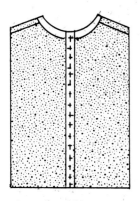

sew shoulder seams
bind neck

SEW SHOULDER seam. Finish neck opening with bias binding.

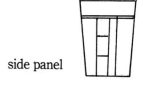

side panel

CUT TWO SIDE panels in underlining fabric and piece as for center panels. Do not finish top of side panel. Sleeve will be sewn to top of side panel in this pattern.

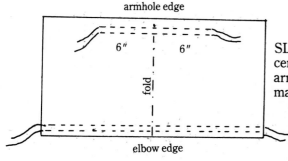

sleeve

SLEEVES are two unlined rectangles cut 12″ long by 24″ wide. Mark center fold line on sleeve. Sew two rows of machine gather stitches on armhole edge for 12″ or 6″ on either side of center mark. Sew two rows of machine gather stitches along elbow edge of sleeve.

CUT OUT TWO cuffs and two linings. Cuff measures 10″ by 3″. Cuff can be altered for personal fit. Sew lining to cuff along one edge. Press seam open.

Gather elbow edge of sleeve to fit cuff. Sew cuff to sleeve. Press gathers down at cuff seam.

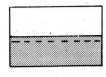

cuff

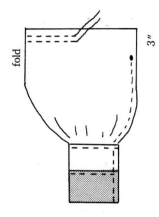

cuff and sleeve

FOLD SLEEVE right sides together along center fold line. Sew underarm sleeve seam along with cuff and cuff lining. Stop sewing sleeve seam 3″ before armhole edge. Leave sleeve seam open half the width of the top of side panel. This part of sleeve will be sewn to top of side panel.

Fold lining on cuff up over cuff and hand hem over gathered seam. This covers raw seam edge. Turn sleeve right side out.

SEW TOP ON SIDE PANEL to unsewn edge of underarm sleeve. Open underarm sleeve seam flat and pin top of side panel to sleeve seam. Stitch from each side of underarm seam to edge. See drawing in little jacket pattern.

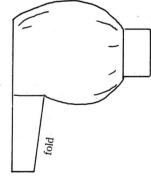

side and sleeve unit

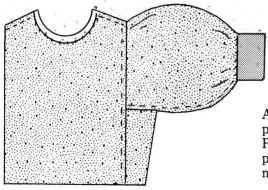

assemble blouse

ASSEMBLE BLOUSE by sewing side panel and sleeve unit to center panel. Pin shoulder fold line of sleeve to shoulder seam of center panel. Pin lower edge of side panel to lower edge of center panel. Continue pinning unit in place. Adjust gathers to fit sleeve into armhole. There is no binding covering this seam.

Finish lower edge of blouse with straight grain binding.

# Long Sleeve Jacket

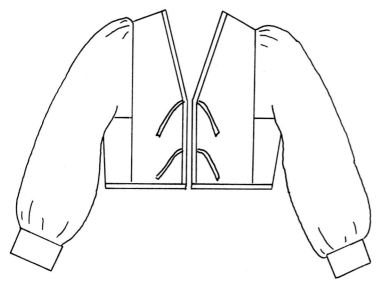

This jacket is the basic vest pattern with long sleeves added to make a jacket. The neck opening is v-shaped. The sleeves are made from a square which is gathered at shoulder and cuff. The jacket is strip pieced to an underlining. See sample jacket on page 21.

**TO DETERMINE FABRIC NEEDED:** this jacket is waist length and can be made from 1/2 yard of fabric for the outside, 1/2 yard of underlining and 1/2 yard of lining. Additional 1/2 yard is needed for bias binding to cover raw edges. Allow one yard of fabric for sleeves and one yard for optional sleeve lining. If jacket is strip pieced, small amounts of different fabrics for piecing are necessary. See directions for strip piecing on page 4.

**TO DETERMINE JACKET SIZE:** the measurements in this book are for a medium size. To change the pattern size for personal fit follow directions on page 3.

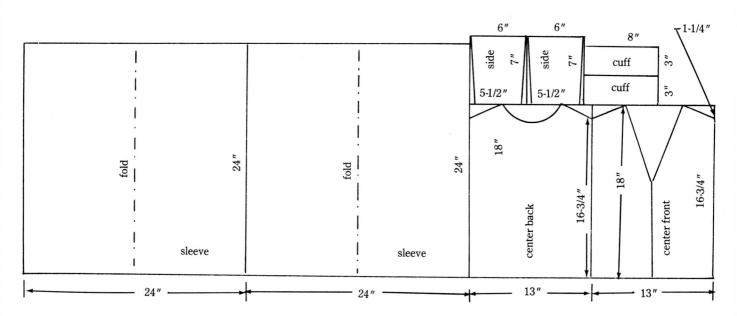

**DIMENSIONS OF PATTERN PIECES:** center panel has front and back panel 13″ wide by 18″ long sewn together at the shoulder. Shape shoulder 1-1/4″. Add 1/4″ seam allowance to pattern piece for shoulder seam. Neck opening is v-shaped in front and uses the template found in back of book for back neck opening. Neck is finished with bias binding. No seam allowance is necessary on neck edge. Armhole is 9″ from shoulder seam to top of side panel. Side panel length is 9″ shorter than center panel. Size of side panel is 6″ wide by 7″ long. Side panel can be shaped to allow for narrower look at waistline. Medium is 6″ at top and 5-1/2″ at bottom and 7″ long. Sleeve is a 24″ by 24″ square. Sleeve is slightly gathered at shoulder to fit into 9″ deep armhole. Wrist edge of sleeve is gathered to a cuff.

**ADD 1/4″ SEAM ALLOWANCE**

To cut out jacket begin with center panel back. Draw rectangle on underlining fabric. Draw rectangle and then trace template for back neck opening in center on top edge. Shape shoulder by drawing from neck opening to armhole edge allowing 1/4″ seam allowance. Repeat for center front. On front underlining draw v-shaped neck opening. Mark middle of front panel. Neck opening is 8″ deep. Mark 8″ down from top of front panel. Shape shoulder seam on front panel matching with shoulder seam on back panel. Draw from right neck edge of shoulder seam to 8″ mark and from left neck edge of shoulder seam to 8″ mark making v-shaped opening. Slash from point of v to hem for front opening.

COVER CENTER BACK panel underlining with strip piecing. Line center back panel with lining fabric. Repeat piecing on center front underlining. Line center front panels.

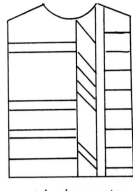

strip piece center back

SEW SHOULDER seams. To finish shoulder seam, sew center back all three layers—pieced layer, underlining, lining to center front two layers—pieced layer, underlining. Hand sew the front panel lining over shoulder seam.

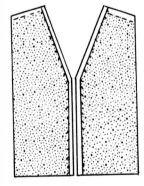

sew shoulders
bind neck opening
and fronts

BIND CENTER front and around neck opening with bias binding. See General Directions on page 3. If ties are desired as front closure, add ties in binding seam. Ties are 6″ long and cut from 1-1/2″ wide strip of fabric finished to 1/2″ wide.

CUT TWO SIDE panels in underlining fabric. Piece as for center panels. Line side panels. Do not finish top of side panels. Sleeve will be sewn to top of side panel in this jacket.

side panel

SLEEVES are two unlined squares 24″ by 24″. Mark center fold line on sleeve. Sew two rows of machine gather stitches on armhole edge for 12″ or 6″ on either side of center mark. Sew two rows of machine gather stitches along wrist edge of sleeve. Sleeve may be lined if desired. Cut lining same as sleeve. Follow directions in little jacket pattern for lining sleeve.

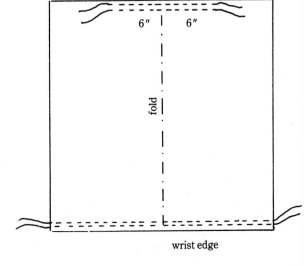

armhole edge

6″    6″

fold

wrist edge

sleeve

CUT OUT TWO cuffs and two linings. Add seam allowance. Cuff measures 8″ wide by 3″ long. Cuff should be large enough for hand to slip through. Sew lining to cuff along one edge. Press seam open.

Gather wrist edge of sleeve to fit cuff. Sew cuff to sleeve. Press gathers down at cuff seam.

cuff

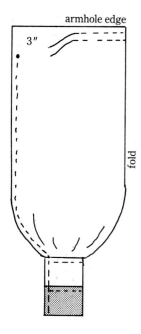

sleeve and cuff

FOLD SLEEVE RIGHT sides together along center fold line. Sew underarm sleeve seam along with cuff and cuff lining. Stop sewing sleeve seam 3″ before armhole edge. Leave sleeve seam open half the width of the top of side panel. This part of sleeve will be sewn to top of side panel.

Fold lining on cuff up over cuff and hand hem lining over gathered seam. This covers raw seam edge. Turn sleeve right side out.

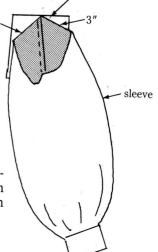

sew sleeve to side panel

SEW TOP OF side panel to unsewn edge of underarm sleeve. Open underarm sleeve seam flat and pin top of side panel to sleeve seam. Stitch from each side of underarm seam to edge.

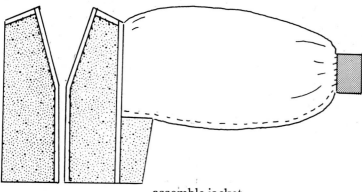

assemble jacket

ASSEMBLE JACKET by sewing side panel and sleeve unit to center panel. Pin shoulder fold line of sleeve to shoulder seam of jacket. Pin lower edge of side panel to lower edge of center panel. Continue pinning unit in place. Adjust gathers to fit sleeve into armhole. Sew bias binding over this joining seam.

Finish lower edge of jacket with straight grain binding.

# Over Jacket

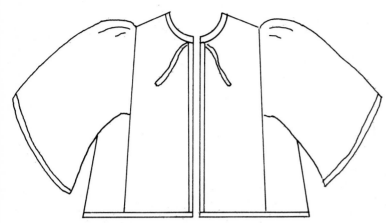

This jacket is adapted from the basic vest pattern. In this pattern the center front and back panels and side panels have been widened and lengthened. The sleeves are like those of little jacket but are narrower. Sample jacket is strip pieced to a lightweight lining. There is no underlining. Sleeves are lined. This jacket can be worn over the basic vest. See sample jacket on page 20.

TO DETERMINE FABRIC NEEDED: the jacket length is 3″ below the waist and can be made from 1-1/4 yards of fabric for outside and 1-1/4 yards for lining. Additional 1/2 yard is needed for bias binding to cover raw edges. Allow 2/3 yard of fabric for outside sleeve and 2/3 yard fabric for sleeve lining. If jacket is strip pieced, small amounts of different fabrics for piecing are necessary. See directions for strip piecing on page 4.

TO DETERMINE JACKET SIZE: the measurements in this book are for a medium size. To change the pattern size for personal fit follow directions on page 3.

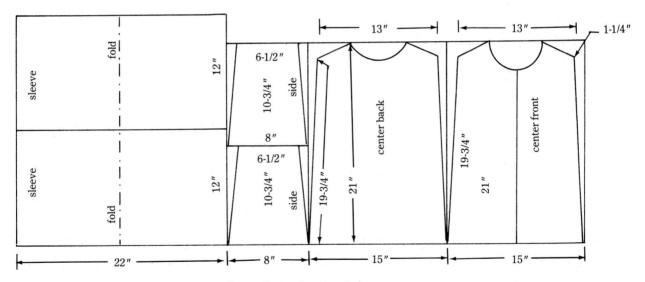

dimensions of pattern pieces

DIMENSIONS OF PATTERN PIECES: center panel has front and back panel cut from 21″ long by 15″ wide rectangle. Center panels are shaped to 13″ at top by 15″ at bottom by 21″ long. Shape shoulders 1-1/4″. Add 1/4″ seam allowance to pattern piece for shoulder seam. Neck opening is from template found in back of book. It is finished with a bias binding. No seam allowance is necessary on neck edge. Armhole is 9″ from shoulder seam to top of side panel. Side panel length is 9″ shorter than center panel. Side panel is 6-1/2″ wide at top by 8-1/2″ wide at bottom, and 10-3/4″ long. Sleeve is a rectangle 12″ wide by 22″ long. The sleeve is slightly gathered at shoulder to fit into 9″ deep armhole.

ADD 1/4″ SEAM ALLOWANCE

Pattern continues on page 30.

**I.** **Short Sleeve Coat**
*Trio.* Coat is patchwork, batted and hand quilted. Jacket is variation of long sleeve pattern strip pieced to underlining.
Gathered skirt with patchwork border.
Coat pattern on page 34.

**J.**

**J.** **Long Vest**
*Lancaster.* Strip pieced to under-
lining, lined in denim.
Pattern on page 32.

**K.**

**K.** **Basic Vest with Patchwork**
*Safflower.* Patchwork, batted and
hand quilted.
Pattern on page 8.

Over Jacket continued.

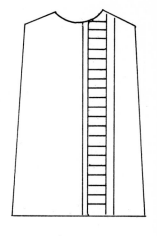

To cut out jacket begin with center panel back. Draw rectangle on lining fabric. Draw rectangle and then shape panel as shown in pattern pieces. Trace template for back neck opening in center on top edge. Shape shoulder by drawing from neck opening to armhole edge allowing 1/4″ seam allowance. Repeat for center front. Slash center front for front opening after drawing neck opening. Jacket edges just meet in front. There is no overlap.

COVER CENTER BACK PANEL lining with strip piecing. Repeat on center front lining.

strip piece center back

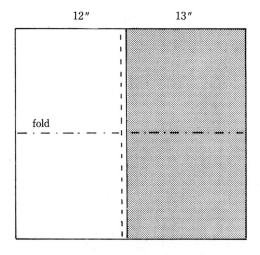

BIND CENTER FRONT raw edges with straight grain binding. See General Directions on page 3. If ties are desired as front closure, add ties in binding seam. Ties are 6″ long and cut from 1-1/2″ wide strip of fabric finished to 1/2″ wide.

Sew shoulder seams. Finish shoulder seam with binding.

Finish neck opening with bias binding.

bind center front
sew shoulder seams
bind neck edge

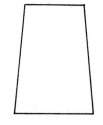

side panel

CUT TWO SIDE panels of fabric and lining fabric. Handle two layers as one. Do not finish top of side panel. Sleeve will be sewn to top of side panel in this jacket.

12″        13″

fold

sleeve and lining

SLEEVES are two rectangles cut 12″ long by 22″ wide. The lining of the sleeve extends 1/4″ below the sleeve. Cut lining 1″ longer than sleeve, 13″ by 22″. Sleeve is gathered at center to fit into 9″ deep armhole.

Sew sleeve and lining together along elbow edge. Press sleeve seam flat toward lining so lining will fold over seam allowance. With right sides together fold sleeve and lining on shoulder fold line.

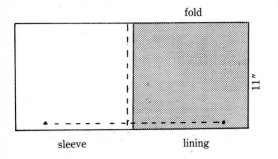

fold

11"

sleeve          lining

sew underarm seam

Sew underarm sleeve seam in center leaving both ends of sleeve and lining seam open.

LEAVE SEAM OPEN half the width of top of side panel. If side panel is 6-1/2" at top, leave seam open 3-1/4" on either end of underarm seam. Press seam open.

TURN SLEEVE AND lining so wrong sides are together. Pin armhole edge of sleeve and lining together. Mark shoulder fold line on sleeve. Sew two rows of machine gather stitches along armhole edge of sleeve to total of 12" or 6" on each side of shoulder fold line.

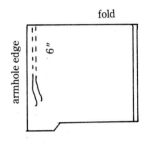

fold

6"

armhole edge

gather sleeve

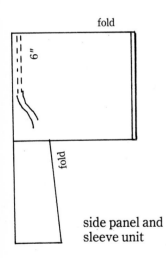

fold

6"

fold

side panel and sleeve unit

SEW TOP OF side panel to unsewn edge of underarm sleeve. *Sew Side panel to sleeve fabric only.* Do not sew sleeve lining in this seam. Sleeve lining is *hand sewn* over machine seam to finish underarm seam. To sew seam, open underarm sleeve seam flat and pin top of side panel to sleeve seam. Stitch from each side of underarm seam to edge. Sew lining by hand over machine seam. See drawing in little jacket pattern.

ASSEMBLE JACKET by sewing side panel and sleeve unit to center panel. Pin shoulder fold line of sleeve to shoulder seam of jacket. Pin lower edge of side panel to lower edge of center panel. Continue pinning unit in place. Adjust gathers to fit sleeve into armhole. Sew bias binding over this joining seam.

Finish lower edge of jacket with straight grain binding.

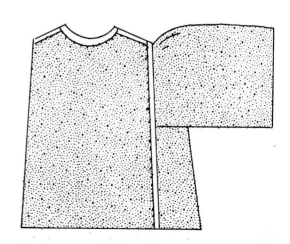

assemble jacket

# Long Vest

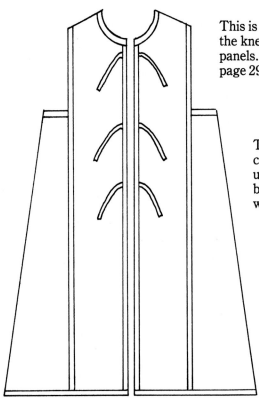

This is a long vest adapted from the basic vest. This pattern comes below the knee. The vest consists of a center panel front and back and two side panels. Sample vest is strip pieced to an underlining. See sample vest on page 29.

TO DETERMINE FABRIC NEEDED: the vest is below the knee and can be made from 2-1/4 yards of fabric for the outside and 2-1/4 yards for underlining and 2-1/4 yards for lining. Additional 2/3 yard is needed for bias binding to cover raw edges. If vest is strip pieced, additional fabrics will be necessary. See directions for strip piecing on page 4.

TO DETERMINE VEST SIZE: the measurements in this book are for a medium size. To change the pattern size for personal fit follow directions on page 3. In the long vest the side panel lower edge width (13″) is the same as the center panel width (13″).

DIMENSIONS OF PATTERN PIECES: center panel has front and back panel 13″ wide by 40″ long sewn together at the shoulder. Shape shoulder seam 1-1/4″. Add 1/4″ seam allowance to pattern piece for shoulder seam. Neck opening is from template found in back of book. It is finished with bias binding. No seam allowance is necessary on neck edge. Armhole is 9″ from shoulder seam to top of side panel. Side panel length is 9″ shorter than center panel. Width of side panel is 6″ wide at top and 13″ wide at bottom and 30″ long.

**ADD 1/4″ SEAM ALLOWANCE**

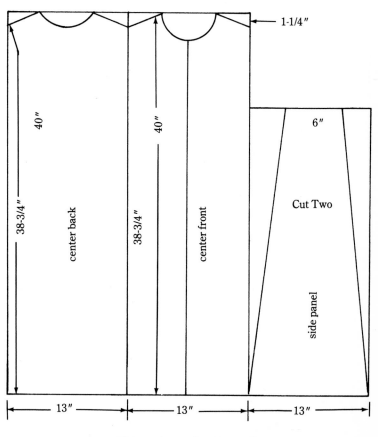

dimensions of pattern pieces

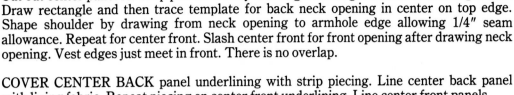

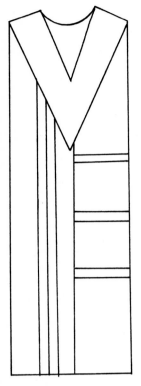

Cut out center panel for strip pieced vest by drawing a rectangle on the underlining fabric. Draw rectangle and then trace template for back neck opening in center on top edge. Shape shoulder by drawing from neck opening to armhole edge allowing 1/4" seam allowance. Repeat for center front. Slash center front for front opening after drawing neck opening. Vest edges just meet in front. There is no overlap.

**COVER CENTER BACK** panel underlining with strip piecing. Line center back panel with lining fabric. Repeat piecing on center front underlining. Line center front panels.

Bind center front raw edges with straight grain binding. See General Directions on page 3. If ties are desired as front closure, add ties in binding seam. Ties are 6" long and cut from 1-1/2" wide strip of fabric finished to 1/2" wide.

Sew shoulder seams. To finish shoulder seam, sew center back all three layers—pieced layer, underlining, lining to center panel two layers—pieced layer, underlining. Hand sew the front panel lining over shoulder seam.

Finish neck opening with bias binding.

strip piece center
back

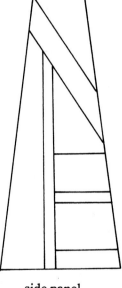

CUT TWO SIDE panels in underlining fabric and piece as for center panels. Line side panels. Finish top of side panels with straight grain binding.

side panel

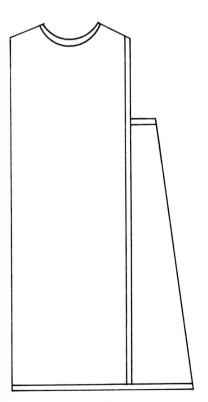

ASSEMBLE VEST by sewing side panels to center panel with bias binding over seam. Binding can be decorative on outside of vest or sewn on lining side. For outside binding pin with lining sides together. Pin side panels to center panel starting at lower edge. For inside binding pin with outsides together. This binding also finishes the armhole.

Finish lower edge of vest with straight grain binding.

assemble vest

# Short Sleeve Coat

The patterns in VARIATIONS are all interchangeable. This coat is adapted from long vest pattern with sleeves from little jacket pattern. The coat can be strip pieced to an underlining as in the sample on page 5. The coat can also be made in patchwork, batted and hand quilted as in the sample on page 28.

TO DETERMINE FABRIC NEEDED: follow instructions for long vest pattern on page 32 adding 2/3 yard fabric for sleeve and 2/3 yard for lining.

To assemble coat please follow instructions found in little jacket pattern on page 10.

The Short Sleeve Coat featured on page 28 has a long sleeve jacket and gathered skirt under the coat to make an outfit called *Trio*. The jacket is from the basic vest pattern with long fitted sleeves added. The sleeves were a long rectangle shaped to narrow at the wrist edge. Since no allowance was made for the bend of the elbow on the sleeve, this pattern tends to be tight through the back underarm when the arm is bent. For this reason the long sleeve should be altered to allow for elbow bend.

The gathered skirt shown on page 28 with *Trio* was designed to match the patchwork in the coat and the strip piecing of the jacket. A band was made in patchwork and attached to a skirt. The width of the skirt should be the same as the width of lower edge of coat. The skirt can be made longer than the coat to add a narrow border under the coat.

ADD 1/4″ SEAM ALLOWANCE

# Long Sleeve Coat

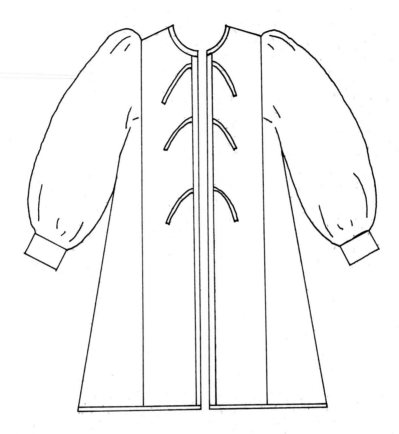

Additional variations can be made from these patterns. This coat is adapted from long vest pattern with sleeves from long sleeve jacket pattern. The coat can be strip pieced to an underlining or done in patchwork and batted with hand quilting. Sample coat on page 36 is patchwork, lined and hand quilted.

TO DETERMINE FABRIC NEEDED: follow instructions for long vest pattern adding fabric requirements for long sleeve pattern.

To assemble coat please follow instructions found in long sleeve jacket pattern on page 24.

ADD 1/4" SEAM ALLOWANCE

**L.**

**L.    Long Sleeve Coat**
*Memories*. Patchwork, batted and hand quilted. Chevron stripe hand pieced.
Pattern on page 35.

# Additional Pattern Ideas

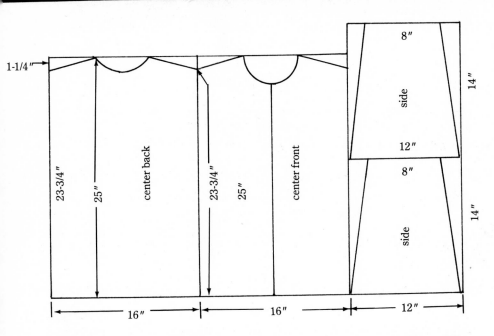

One of the vests modeled on the back cover is done in a large size. The dimensions of pattern pieces have been modified. Assembling vest is the same as for basic vest with patchwork pattern.

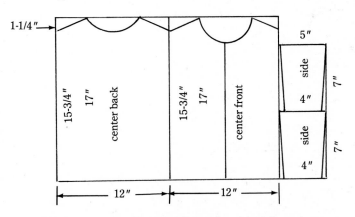

Dimensions of pattern pieces for a small vest are as follows in the drawing. Assembling the vest is the same as basic vest pattern.

## FOR MEN

The basic vest can also be altered to fit men. Follow directions for changing pattern size on page 3. Men have larger shoulders than women and sometimes are proportionately narrower in the waist. Make the armhole larger for ease of fit on a man. Consideration must be taken in choice of fabrics for men. Standard colors in male attire are blue, brown, rust, green, grey and burgundy. Know your subject before making choice of color. The scale of prints should be medium to large and generally geometric rather than floral in design.

# Template

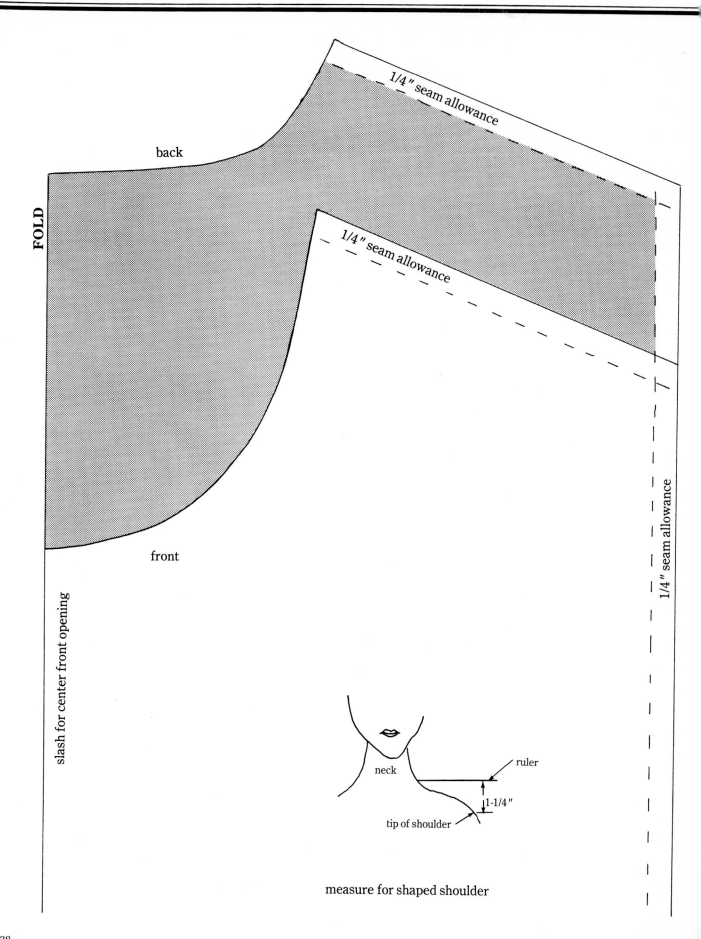

1/4" seam allowance

back

FOLD

1/4" seam allowance

front

slash for center front opening

1/4" seam allowance

neck

ruler

1-1/4"

tip of shoulder

measure for shaped shoulder

# Bibliography

Da Conceicao, Maria, *Wearable Art*, Penguin Books, N.Y., 1979.
Gutcheon, Beth, *The Perfect Patchwork Primer*, Penguin Books, N.Y., 1973.
Gutcheon, Beth and Jeffrey, *The Quilt Design Workbook*, Rawson Publishers, Inc., N.Y., 1976.
James, Michael, *The Quiltmakers Handbook*, Prentice-Hall, Inc., N.J., 1978.
James, Michael, *The Second Quiltmakers Handbook,* Prentice-Hall, Inc., N.J., 1981
Johannah, Barbara, *The Quick Quiltmakers Handbook*, Pride of the Forest Press, CA., 1979.
Leone, Diana, *The Sampler Quilt*, Leone Publications, CA., 1980.
Porcella, Yvonne, *Pieced Clothing*, Porcella Studios, CA., 1980.
Sunset Books, *Quilting*, Lane Publishing, CA., 1981.

## ACKNOWLEDGEMENTS

A book such as this takes lots of work and dedication. It could not be done without the aid of a few of my very best friends who lend support and guidance. A book such as this takes lots of time and energy to put everything together. My family suffers along with me and I thank them for their patience.

Front Cover: Transition of Basic Vest into *Variations*.
Basic Vest, Blouse and Little Jacket.
Back Cover: Author and family wearing *Variations* made from patterns in this book.

For additional copies of *PIECED CLOTHING, VARIATIONS, FIVE ETHNIC PATTERNS* and *PLUS FIVE* or information on workshops contact:
Yvonne Porcella
3619 Shoemake Ave.
Modesto, CA 95351